BORN TO PULL

stories by **Bob Cary**

illustrations by **Gail de Marcken**

SCHOLASTIC INC.

New York Toronto London Auckland Sydney
Mexico City New Delhi Hong Kong Buenos Aires

Editorial Development: Casey McGee, Michelle Ethun
Art Director: Joy Morgan Dey

ISBN 0-439-28682-4

12 11 10 9 8 7 6 5 4 3 2 1   1 2 3 4 5 6/0

Printed in the U.S.A.   24

First Scholastic printing, October 2001

This book is dedicated to all the mushers, sled dog handlers, veterinarians, and fans who nurture and love the world's greatest athletes—the sled dogs.

Special thanks to the following mushers for sharing their personal insights and stories: Myron Angstman, Don and Val Beland, Mark Black, Steve Crittendon, Sue Hendrickson and Paul Schurke, Patty Holmberg, Craig Johnson, Bob Klaesges, Dan and Vicki Kondos, Harry and Mary Lambirth, Jamie Nelson, Stu and Michelle Osthoff, Will Steger, John and Shelly Stetson, and Norman Vaughan.

—Bob Cary

Special thanks to Val and Don Beland, Gail and Lucas Branstrom, Joe Chambers, Paya de Marcken, Peter McClelland, Paul Reigert, Paul Schurke, and Paul Sletten.

—Gail de Marcken

Special thanks to the staff and volunteers of the John Beargrease Sled Dog Marathon, who provided invaluable technical support and guidance: Peter Furo, Brian Patterson, and Patty Pruden.

—Pfeifer-Hamilton Staff

Humans and dogs have held a close relationship dating back thousands of years—far beyond recorded history. Our oldest ancestors raised wolf pups, crossbred those which could be domesticated, and purposely evolved canines to act as guardians, hunters,

There are times, they note, while running down a snow-packed forest trail on a still, star-studded night, when this magic inevitably takes over.

Perhaps it is magnified by the distant, unmistakable cry of a hunting wolf pack—an

Beyond the Frozen Edge

herders, and haulers. Some Native Americans are convinced that dogs are the bridge between the "four-legged" animals such as wolves and deer and the "two-legged" animals—humans. With their unique connection to both worlds, sled dogs unmistakably fit this belief.

Veteran mushers, at those rare times when they choose to bare their innermost thoughts, universally reveal that their relationship with their dogs is as close as any relationship they know, sometimes even closer than their relationships with other people. They say that a sled dog team will take you to the edge of another place—a mystical place which you cannot enter, but which you may be lucky enough to glimpse; a place larger, more real, and more beautiful than any you have imagined; a place nearly impossible to describe.

eerie, exultant, primordial exchange in which the musher becomes immersed.

Or perhaps it is simply the silence, the solitude, and the soft, long blue shadows interspersed with pale yellow patches of moonlight rolling past beneath the runners, mile after mile, that bonds the dog team and musher into a physical, mental, and spiritual union.

Whatever it is, this is dog sledding at its mystical best. And as long as there are dogs born to pull and people driven by a spark of adventure, the two will inevitably be drawn together on the snowpack.

This book is a celebration of those exquisite dogs who are truly *Born to Pull.*

CONTENTS

Hike!

The command that tells the dog team, "Let's go!"

Sled Dogs

For centuries, until the advent of snowmobiles a mere forty years ago, the people of northern regions—Canada, the northern United States, Lapland, Greenland, Siberia, Chukotka, Norway, and Finland—relied on dog teams for winter travel. Sled dogs pulled them over otherwise impassable distances of snow and ice, protected them from danger, and guided them home through trackless wilderness, never forgetting the way. These burly, strong dogs were the life blood of the northern winter world.

Although many people now use snowmobiles for winter travel, today we see a tremendous resurgence of interest in sled dogs. People from all climates, not just northern regions, are rediscovering the joy and fascination of raising and caring for sled dogs, training dog teams, and running them for pleasure.

TYPES OF SLED DOGS

Malamute
large freight dogs

Siberian husky
medium-build dogs with some racing ability

Inuit/Eskimo dog
stout, hardy dogs from arctic regions

Alaskan husky
mixed-breed dogs, varying size, bred for endurance and for racing performance (also known as **Indian dog**)

7

SIBERIAN HUSKY

broad chests, thick coats, and tough feet. Malamutes weigh between 80 and 120 pounds and have round, soft faces. For these dogs, speed has little or no value and pulling is their primary skill. Freight dogs will eat almost anything. They can survive extremely cold temperatures and pull hard under any conditions. These traits make them invaluable participants in expeditions and long adventure trips.

Siberian huskies, a smaller breed recognizable by mask-like facial features and blue eyes, are also formidable pullers. Pound for pound, Siberians can pull more than Malamutes—but for shorter periods of time. Siberians weigh only 40 to 60 pounds. They are now selectively bred for their traditional appearance as well as for their pulling abilities.

In the last century, as dog team travel has become less of a necessity, the appeal of sophisticated racing and recreational mushing has increased. Accordingly, specialized racing and freight dogs have evolved through selective breeding.

Eskimo dogs, so named because they originated in Greenland, are burly, well-insulated dogs that persevere slowly but surely through arduous extended trips. They are used heavily by mushers who offer dog sled adventures as well as those who undertake long expeditions through remote regions.

Mixed-breed dogs called Alaskan huskies, a cross between the Siberian husky and a surprising assortment of other breeds, are the most common dogs on the racing circuit. This motley "breed" of dogs is so varied that many bear little resemblance to each other or to their husky heritage. Another name used extensively for these hybrids is "Indian dog" because most

Who Are These Dogs?

The image projected by Hollywood and several decades of calendar art depicts the sled dog as either a Siberian husky or a Malamute. Both of these breeds are registered by the American Kennel Club (AKC), and both have distinctive features originating from wolf ancestry.

Malamutes have big, strong physiques and are well-suited for hauling heavy loads. They are included with non-pedigreed, burly dogs in a class called freight dogs, which are known for of the best racing dogs have come out of Indian villages in the Alaskan and Canadian interior.

Alaskan huskies weigh between 40 and 75 pounds and may be thickly furred or somewhat sleek, depending upon their heritage. These dogs are splotched or spotted in an assortment of colors from white to brown to black. Their eyes may be black, blue, or brown. Many mushers have even introduced greyhound blood into their kennels for speed. A few dogs have a smidgen of wolf in their not-too-distant ancestry, giving them the endurance wolves need in the wild. The exact amount of wolf ancestry is difficult to determine. Since wolf-dog mixes can be notoriously unpredictable and difficult, many mushers refuse to talk about this element of their breeding strategy.

Although sled dog teams have also included Irish setters, German shorthair pointers, Labrador retrievers, hounds, and terriers, the Alaskan husky is the only dog selectively bred purely for pulling.

Dog trainers with a good eye for detail can determine some of the varied ancestry of Alaskan huskies just by looking. Although these speedy canines are not recognized as a pure breed by the AKC, the lack of official approval is of little consequence to the people who run and race these dogs. Mushers place greater importance on the accomplishments of the parents: how hard they pulled and how many wins they produced.

MALAMUTE

Malamutes and other burly freight dogs are the Mack trucks of the sled dog world.

SIBERIAN HUSKY

This widely-recognized, traditional masked face belongs to the Siberian husky. Today, most purebred Siberians are show dogs. While they can be good runners, this American Kennel Club-approved breed has been selected more for appearance than for performance. As a result, not many of today's purebred Siberians are able to run great distances while pulling a sled.

It is the rare team that includes a dog with no husky in its bloodline.

Sizes and Styles

Sled dogs are bred specifically for strength, speed, endurance, intelligence, a willingness to follow orders, and a desire to pull. The best racing dogs, therefore, have a heritage marked more by accomplishment than by breed purity. Notice the variety of coloring patterns that are common in Alaskan huskies.

ALASKAN HUSKY

ALASKAN HUSKY

Sprint racing dogs are sleeker and smaller than freight dogs or long distance racers. Teams of sprint dogs can cover as many as thirty miles in an hour.

Fur

The amount of fur on a sled dog is determined by the dog's function. Freight and expedition dogs, because they are required to spend weeks outdoors in subzero temperatures, grow dense coats of fur. Similarly, sled dogs used in long marathon races like the Iditarod in Alaska or the John Beargrease Sled Dog Marathon in Minnesota, where they must sleep out overnight in frigid conditions, grow heavier coats.

In direct contrast, sprint dogs expend enormous amounts of energy in very short bursts—usually running fewer than two hours at any given time. Their coats are light in both texture and thickness, making it easy for their body heat to escape. Mid-distance runners, naturally, have coats somewhere in between.

11

Mushing for Brook Trout

An orange winter sun, like a huge ball of frozen sherbet, edges up over the eastern rim of the world. In the subzero cold, wisps of vapor drift across the snowpacked surface of Moose Lake in northern Minnesota. It is that moment of dawn when the cracking, expanding ice lets you know that the temperature is the lowest. "Boom! Boom! Boom!" it sounds, approaching like an express train from the far end of the lake. "Boom!…Boom!… BOOM!…BOOM!…BOOM!" It passes almost underfoot, then recedes to the west. "BOOM!… Boom!…boom!" and vanishes.

"Hike, Russell! Hike, Reno!"

Musher Steve Crittendon, age twenty-six, pulls up his snow hook and orders his twin lead dogs into action. He is followed by six other Minnesotans on skis, ranging in age from twenty to seventy, who are following an established north country tradition. It is January 1, opening day of the winter trout season, and they are heading for a remote lake along the Minnesota-Ontario border.

Luckily, the trail has already been packed by previous mushers. This winter, a heavy snow has pressed down the ice covering the lake and forced water up through cracks. The result is a six-inch layer of soft slush that remains unfrozen, insulated from the cold by a mantle of fluffy snow. On the trail, the slush is frozen solid, but woe unto anyone who wanders off that packed trail! A dog sled mired in slush is difficult to pull, and accumulating ice on the runners only aggravates the situation. A skier who plunges into slush will find his skis turning into huge, unmanageable clumps of ice—a trip to shore and tedious scraping are required to continue the trip. The group gives silent thanks to the mushers who went ahead, broke trail, and made the journey infinitely easier.

Mile after mile of sparkling snow falls behind, and eventually they arrive at the partially-obscured, snow-laden portage trail that leads two hundred yards to the small trout lake. The team pushes out onto the unbroken surface, aware that no one has been here ahead of them. They have this entire remote trout lake to themselves!

The dogs are tethered, the sleds unloaded. Ski boots are exchanged for mukluks and sweaters for parkas. Several group members, having fished this lake by canoe in the summer, know the underwater structure and drill holes over a sunken, weedy sand bar.

Anglers drop shiny metal lures into the dark depths and are rewarded almost immediately by heavy tugs on their lines. Thick-bodied, red-finned brook trout fight furiously against being brought to the surface. By noon, eight trophies, from fourteen to eighteen inches long, are flopping on the ice. Another four trout somehow escape and remain free in the black water.

The dogs stare impassively at the fishing activities while they lounge in the full sun, only occasionally playing lazily with each other.

In the shelter of some shoreline pines, the travelers kick the loose snow down to solid ground and kindle a fire. In moments, a bucket of bratwurst boils on the flames while a pot of coffee steams to one side. Stories of other winter trout trips mingle with the wood smoke.

Lunch over, they kick snow onto the fire to make sure it is out. Ski boots replace mukluks, and sweaters replace parkas. They load up the dog sleds and push back over the portage to the packed trail. Aware they are now heading for home where dinner and warm beds await, the dogs plunge ahead with renewed zest.

The waning sun casts a final golden glow on the tips of the forested hills as the team pulls into the wilderness access point where vehicles are parked. The group pauses for a moment on the blue-tinted snow just to absorb the scene before slipping off skis and unharnessing the dogs. It has been one of those magic north country winter days that are etched forever in memory.

ALASKAN HUSKY

Quick, lightweight, thin-haired dogs are used mainly in sprint racing teams that stay on the course only for short periods of time.

14 *Hike!* **SLED DOGS**

Jamie's "Elite Mutts"

Many sled dogs are bought simply by virtue of their parents' racing accomplishments. Over the years Jamie Nelson, a long-distance marathon musher from northern Minnesota, has developed a distinct strain of dogs. Even though she refers to them as elite mutts, other mushers have been eager to purchase the long-legged, powerful dogs from her kennel. She has specifically bred her dogs to her personal performance ideal by mating selected sires and dams that offer the right physical and temperamental qualities she desires. Of course, Jamie Nelson is not alone. Every musher carefully develops the performance characteristics of his or her own kennel.

15

North to the Pole

In 1986, television viewers across North America watched in fascination as the Steger North Pole Expedition successfully closed in on its goal. It was a venture by five men, one woman, and forty-nine tenacious sled dogs to reach the North Pole on foot, unsupported by outside assistance. The international team, led by Will Steger and Paul Schurke from Ely, Minnesota, came home to jubilant acclaim. Both leaders went on to further exploration—Will to the South Pole and Paul to Russia.

Champions

They came to the finish line of the five hundred-mile John Beargrease Sled Dog Marathon with heads up and tails wagging—twelve of Jamie Nelson's best sled dogs, headed by leaders Arctic and Hickory. Four dogs of the starting team of sixteen had been taken out of the harness along the way, but the twelve that finished did so with style and the pride of their breeding.

Tears of appreciation filled Jamie's eyes as she crossed the finish line in Duluth, Minnesota. "These are the elite dogs of muttdom!" she laughed.

For sure, none of the twelve can be found listed in the American Kennel Club registry, but they are thoroughbreds nonetheless. Their ancestry harkens back to centuries of sled dogs, bred and crossbred by Native Americans living on the rim of the Arctic. And they had just brought the Togo, Minnesota, musher her third Beargrease winner's trophy.

"I almost talked my team out of the finish," Nelson confessed later. "The dogs have excellent memories, and they remembered clearly the race start at Ordean Junior High School. When we hit the final stretch, I yelled at them: 'OK! Let's go home!' and home they went. But 'home' to them was the Ordean athletic field. When we came to the cutoff, they kept wanting to go straight back to the starting line. I had a heck of a time getting them stopped and aimed down the right road, but we finally got our communications worked out and came in running at full speed."

After receiving the deserved accolades at a colorful victory banquet, the three-time Beargrease winner headed home to Togo with her awards: a $10,000 cash purse and a new Chevrolet truck. She put the cash towards paying off some of her kennel bills and traveling expenses. But the truck she offered on loan to a friend.

During the course of the race she had heard that another musher, Harry Lambirth, was experiencing motor trouble with his dog truck.

"When she got home she phoned to ask if I would like to use the new Chevrolet until I could get my truck fixed," Harry recounted. "I thanked her, but told her my truck was now running fine. It is so typical of Jamie to be concerned about another musher. It is one of the characteristics that makes her a unique sled dog champion."

The Pope and the Devil

It is nearly impossible to talk for very long about sled dogs without bringing up the name of Alaskan musher and author Norman Vaughan, the man who handled Admiral Richard E. Byrd's dog teams on the 1929 Expedition into Antarctica. At age ninety, he was still going strong on a recent winter day in the wood-heated headquarters of Paul Schurke's Wintergreen operation on White Iron Lake near Ely, Minnesota. White-haired and white-bearded, Vaughan was holding forth with some winter campers inside the warm interior while the thermometer on the outside porch headed down to 40° below zero.

His blue eyes twinkled as he loosened up the fur collar of his parka and recounted to the group an endless array of adventures that covered dog sledding, mountain climbing, and a stint with a U.S. Army search and rescue unit in World War II.

"Did I ever tell you about the time I took Pope John Paul II on a dog sled ride?" he asked. Before anyone could answer, he continued. "When the Pope was scheduled to visit Anchorage in 1981, I suggested to the welcoming committee that we give him a ride in a dog sled."

Vaughan laughed, savoring the memory. "There was a lot of concern about security, and the Secret Service had a hundred agents on hand. For safety, I had a handler with a control line on each dog to trot alongside the sled.

"When the plane arrived and the Pope stepped down on the runway, I had the dog team ready. I asked John Paul if His Holiness would like to drive a dog team, and he nodded his assent.

"I showed him how to stand on the runners and grip the handle bars. Then, I pointed out to the Pope that I had two dogs with names of which he might not approve—Satan and the Devil—but he just laughed, and the dogs took off. When we got back to the airplane ramp, he turned and blessed the crowd and then blessed the dog team. Probably the only time a Pope ever blessed Satan and the Devil."

Hike! **SLED DOGS**

FAMOUS SLED DOGS

Balto

Nanook

Granite

Ellesmere

Rohn

Zap

Names

Some mushers say the best dog names are single syllables with sharp consonants, making them easily distinguishable when shouted over the heads of a team. Others forsake utility for nostalgia—choosing names of famous predecessors or historical locations (Nanook, Yukon, Tundra). Still others, hard-pressed to come up with an original name for the sixty-seventh dog in the kennel, will call up themes for entire litters such as trees, cars, or American presidents.

ELLESMERE

Home Life

Gee!

The command that tells
the team to turn right

Mushing is not just a sport, it's a way of life. Sled dog kennels are likely to have forty to fifty dogs in residence at any one time. For a musher, this obligation is like owning a dairy farm—the chores of feeding, cleaning up, and training require daily attention with little or no time off. With each dog consuming about $500 in food every year, most mushers must earn a living by taking a traditional job.

Dog sledding is a passion that becomes a life-style and creates a culture. Why? Ask any musher and you'll get virtually the same answer—for the joy of developing the indescribable bond with dogs who become your family and friends. Many mushers report that traveling behind a dog team is a spiritual experience. It provides moments of exhilaration and offers a connection with nature that is incomparable to any other mode of transportation. By means of an intricate blend of control and trust, a team of dogs can safely take the musher to a place he could not go alone.

Living with Sled Dogs

Mushers estimate that it takes a kennel of thirty adult dogs to form a team of twenty dogs ready to race at any given time. This number of dogs prevents a musher from living in a city. In an urban area, zoning regulations usually impose limits of two to three animals per family. So, for legal as well as aesthetic reasons, most mushers live out in the country.

Tethering

Mushers very commonly stake out sled dogs by using four- to six-foot swivel chains on posts near the dog houses. Sled dogs are not unhappy when chained. They interact and play with their immediate neighbors and are relatively free to move around.

Housing

Many sled dogs, protected by dense fur coats, live comfortably in areas where winter temperatures regularly drop below zero—sometimes to extremes of 50° or 60° below. Dog houses, roughly-constructed plywood or plastic shelters, serve as important protection from the worst of these elements, keeping out the wind and snow. The door is cut just large enough to allow the dog to pass through, so the temperature inside stays at least 30° above conditions outside. Fresh straw insulates the house and also makes it comfortable. Despite these comforts, some dogs forego the house altogether, even in the severest of storms, in order to sleep outside with their tails curled around their noses.

Fenced-in kennels are used sparingly and are usually reserved for females in heat or puppies under ten months of age.

Kids

It is safe for adults to walk into a dog yard, but it's not wise for small children to wander in alone. Kids are nearly the same size as the dogs and can easily be knocked down by the sheer enthusiasm of the dogs' greeting. If they are not familiar with dogs, children can also unwittingly tease or antagonize them.

Running Away

Sled dogs have a natural roaming instinct and are known to get loose and run off for brief adventures. Although they usually return, they can be absent for a couple of hours or up to a full week. Accidental litters are often the result.

HOME LIFE

At Home

Home life provides an easygoing, relaxed time for sled dogs, who frequently interact and play games with each other or take a moment for an inspired group howl. Individual dogs exhibit strikingly different personalities and can be quite inventive in their games, such as passing sticks just out of reach of a neighboring dog or capturing another dog's empty food bowl. Older sled dogs even baby-sit puppies, allowing the youngsters to romp and chew on them mercilessly.

When not racing or working, dogs sleep
a lot—sometimes up to eighteen
hours a day. They seem to enjoy
a patient life of leisure that most
people would consider boring.

Built-in Compasses

Many mushers believe that dogs have a sixth sense about where they are and in what direction they are headed. When riding home from a race, even from several hundred miles away, dogs usually sleep in their boxes until the truck is a half mile or so from their home. Then, they become wide awake and start barking in anticipation of their arrival.

There's No Place Like Home...

Myron Angstman, an Alaskan musher, likes to relate an intriguing story about Hot Foot, the lead dog of the first team to win the Iditarod race. Hot Foot was born and raised in Stony River, Alaska. One winter, Myron loaned him to another team—but after that year's Iditarod race ended in Nome, the dog apparently got a bad case of homesickness. He escaped from the dog yard and vanished, much to the consternation and embarrassment of the other musher. The following May, Hot Foot appeared home in Stony River, having traveled cross-country over six hundred miles.

Food, Glorious Food!

Sled dogs are athletes, first and foremost. Like their human counterparts, their bodies must be kept in peak condition. They must eat well every day, and their usual diet must be supplemented with customized meals during special events.

The rigors of training and living outdoors in subzero temperatures also call for a special diet. Since many mushers believe that raw meat is essential for proper nutrition, they acquire deer, mink, sheep, fish, beaver carcasses—even the occasional dead cow or horse—for the dogs' daily meals.

Extreme cold, long runs, and harsh racing conditions cause the dogs to burn a huge number of calories. During the racing season, dogs eat a high-fat stew made of raw meat, special dry food, and vitamin supplements. Adding lard to the food mixture also helps the dogs retain their fatty insulation layer—a survival necessity.

All but the most famous (and wealthy) mushers must make difficult decisions about what they feed their kennel. Since money is always a limiting factor, some mushers cannot afford to feed meat throughout the summer. Successful mushers who gain some notoriety occasionally win the sponsorship of corporations, just like in any other professional sport. Sponsors may underwrite the cost of transportation, food, or gear, resulting in fewer cost-related compromises for the musher and kennel. During the racing season, however, no musher skimps on the dogs' food—the fuel that gives them the energy to pull.

True to their wild ancestry, when given the opportunity, sled dogs will capture and eat small birds, grouse, chickens, and even cats.

Water

During the winter, most food is served to sled dogs in liquid form. This helps to increase the dogs' fluid intake. Below-freezing temperatures also require that the water be heated and laced with meat parts or dog food. This entices the dogs to drink it all in a hurry before it freezes.

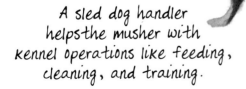

A sled dog handler helps the musher with kennel operations like feeding, cleaning, and training.

Adaptations

In the Arctic, where water is sometimes scarce in liquid form, sled dogs have developed the amazing ability to metabolize fat into the liquid they need to survive. In the "lower north," they must still be encouraged to drink plenty of liquids.

Bad Table Manners

It's true that dogs sometimes eat feces—their own or their neighbor's. No one knows why for sure, but it's possible that undigested nutrients are the attraction. Frequent scooping keeps handlers busy and minimizes this habit that is so offensive to humans.

WHAT DO SLED DOGS EAT?

chicken

beaver

mink

fish

deer

beef

lard

high-protein dog food

Meat

During the winter, meat for the dogs is preserved in nature's outdoor freezer. Handlers use sharp hoes or axes to break off chunks that are brought indoors to thaw. The meat is then mixed with commercial dry food and hot water to make a sloppy stew for the dogs.

Many mushers buy 50-lb. slabs of otherwise unsalable meat parts from plants that process beef, mink, fish, or chicken.

INEDIBLE NOT INTENDED FOR HUMAN FOOD

33

Foot Care

Mushers and handlers take very good care of their sled dogs' feet. For obvious reasons, healthy feet are essential to these fine athletes. The amount and type of care, however, is customized to each dog's activity level and racing style.

Eskimo dogs, native to arctic regions, develop extremely resilient feet with the lowest maintenance needs. They seldom require booties because their foot pads are very tough and don't collect snow.

In contrast, the feet of Alaskan huskies and other breeds with more fur do collect snow between the pads during wet conditions. This makes running difficult and painful for them. Foot booties made of pile or felt, strapped on with velcro, prevent this snow accumulation and protect the feet from minor abrasions. Marathon race organizers frequently require that mushers carry a supply of booties for every dog on their team.

During a race or extended training run, mushers regularly apply salve to the dogs' foot pads to keep them soft and pliant, thus preventing cracks and fissures. Some salves are antibiotic ointments, warding off bacteria and dirt, and reducing swelling. However, these are not allowed during races, as they could be used to mask injuries.

After a race, mushers sometimes wrap their dogs' ankles in sweats. Made of an elastic, woven fabric, sweats look like joint wraps used by human athletes and are applied for the same reason—to prevent swelling.

All dogs, not just sled dogs, require trimmed nails to maintain good posture. During the winter, when sled dogs are most active, their nails require little trimming because they are naturally worn down by the ground's surface. For this reason, trimming becomes a maintenance chore primarily in the summer.

FOOT PROTECTION

booties—keep out snow

salve—prevents chapping, cracks and fissures

ointment—medicinal application

sweats—tendon wraps to prevent post-race swelling

Eskimo Magic

A note of awe creeps into Arctic explorer Paul Schurke's voice and a faraway look comes into his eyes as he relates an incident that occurred during his 1989 Bering Bridge Expedition. The joint Russian-American dog sled venture started on the eastern coast of Siberia, crossed the ice bridge at the Bering Strait and ended up on the western coast of Alaska. Paul and his Russian co-leader were accompanied by Siberian and Alaskan Eskimos and their sled dog teams.

"The Siberian Eskimos had sled dogs that were rough, woolly, and fierce," Paul pointed out. "They stared at me like I was a tender pork chop, and I kept my distance. Those dogs were nothing like our Alaskan or Canadian sled dogs, which tend to be very friendly and easy to get along with."

Paul also noted that he feared for his dogs and at night kept them chained well away from the Siberian dogs. One frigid night, the expedition was bedded down in a small native village in eastern Siberia. Paul was visiting in an Eskimo hut when fierce barking erupted outside. "We ran out to discover ten of the Siberian dogs had broken loose and had piled onto my lead dog, Kohojatak, ripping him into a bloody mess. His stomach was torn open, and some of his intestines had spilled out on the snow. It was horrible, and Kohojatak was in terrible pain. I went to my sled and got my rifle to end his misery, but the Siberian Eskimo men became highly agitated. I could not understand their language, but I could understand that they insisted I not shoot my dog. After some discussion, they carried Kohojatak inside the hut and carefully laid him out on a rug. In a few minutes, an Eskimo shaman appeared in ceremonial garb. He inspected Kohojatak carefully, then cradled the dog in his arms and carried him back outside. I assumed he was going to perform some sort of burial rite."

The next morning, still sad over the loss of his lead dog, Paul got up and prepared to harness his team and move on. The Eskimos, however, would hear none of that. They insisted that the expedition not leave. "Since neither the Russian leader nor I could understand what they were saying, we settled in for another night," Paul explained. "The next day it was the same thing, and I started getting eager to be moving."

The third morning, Paul was awakened by some shouting outside. He went out of the hut to find the same shaman with Kohojatak. Only now the dog was running, jumping and barking.

"I inspected Kohojatak carefully and could hardly tell he had been injured," Paul related. "I have no idea what the shaman did to accomplish such a miracle. The dog had been so badly torn up in the attack, I did not think he would live more than an hour.

"Kohojatak finished the expedition and came home to Minnesota where he lived to pull sleds for three more years. To this day I have no idea how Kohojatak healed so quickly."

Paul shook his head with a distant look. "Siberian Eskimos have been isolated from the rest of the world for generations and have apparently retained many of their old beliefs and methods of healing.

"I often stop to wonder about the old shaman in that remote Eskimo village in eastern Siberia. Even with all of our modern medicine and high technology, there are some things we just do not understand."

Puppies

Mating may occur twice a year when a female dog goes into heat. Gestation lasts sixty-two days (approximately nine weeks). Most mushers, if they have their way, schedule mating in the spring so that the puppies are born and weaned during the summer before cold weather sets in. Litters average five to seven puppies, but they can get as large as thirteen. One litter per year is normally enough for a mother dog since only the best racing females are purposefully bred, and they are needed back on the team as soon as possible!

Puppies are usually born in the late spring so that the mother is ready to run again in the fall.

Birth on the Trail

Paul Schurke owns and operates a wilderness adventure operation, called Wintergreen, in northen Minnesota. At Wintergreen, visitors have the chance to handle a team on short excursions. Guests are mainly urban residents who have seldom—if ever—been around sled dogs, much less ridden a sled. However, once they have practiced the basic techniques of handling a sled and guiding a team by voice commands, they usually do quite well.

"A couple of years ago," Paul recalls, "we had this group on the trail for a lodge-to-lodge trip, mushing all day and spending the nights in cabins. One of the women who was driving a team came from the Deep South. She was a very proper lady, obviously brought up with a strict code of correct speech and behavior. She was driving the dogs, and I was skiing behind.

"I had a small female named Ottawa in this team who was obviously pregnant. I wouldn't have had her pulling except we had all our teams booked out on trips and needed every one of our dogs. She wasn't due to deliver for at least another month—or so we thought.

"In any event, we were on the trail heading for a lodge on Greenstone Lake when the southern lady began to yell, slammed down her brake and tried to slow her dog team. I quickly skied up behind her to see what was happening.

"There is something wrong with that little dog up there!" the lady cried out with obvious embarrassment.

"I skied ahead for a closer look and it was apparent that Ottawa was giving birth right there on the trail. A tiny puppy tumbled out and rolled on the snow as the sled went past. I picked the pup out of the snow, brushed it off, and stuck it inside my parka where it would stay warm, then skied ahead to catch up.

"One of the dogs just gave birth!" I yelled at the startled lady who nodded, hanging grimly onto the sled.

"Here comes another one," she muttered.

"And that wasn't the last. Ottawa gave birth to a total of five pups, each one rolling in the snow, and each one ending up inside my parka. When we got to Greenstone Lake I tied the teams by the lodge and led Ottawa inside where she nursed the pups, who were all healthy.

"Ottawa and her pups came through the experience without any problem, and the pups are now full grown members of my sled dog kennel. I don't really know how the southern lady felt about the experience. She didn't say much, but I bet she took home a story that none of her friends could beat."

Haw!
The command that tells
the team to turn left

Dog Talk

Some cultures believe that dogs form the link between people and the rest of the animal kingdom because they can speak to both worlds. Their senses interpret the outside world better than ours, and their ability to remember surroundings and locations is unparalleled. Perhaps they understand us even better than we understand them.

Dogs pay careful attention to their mushers and handlers, and often anticipate and respond to the unspoken moods of their trainers. Among dogs, communication is very clear and precise—it's just done without words. Facial expressions are very important; dogs use teeth, ears, and head positions to warn us of displeasure, annoyance, and dislike as well as pleasure, tenderness, and deference. Good mushers capitalize on these signs and do not rely simply on verbal commands or physical control. They pay attention to the subtle nuances of body language—the main method of communication for dogs.

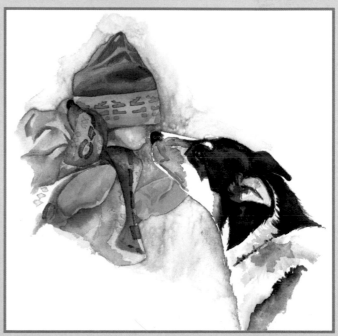

41

Communication

Sled dogs learn the language of communication as youngsters and seem to have an unflagging interest in practicing and playing out their new-found skills with their mother and littermates. Some puppies are naturally **dominant** and are seen as leaders in their social structure, while others are more **submissive** and take direction from their dominant brother or sister.

Like wolf pups, sled dog puppies engage in play and tussling that helps to establish this important social structure and allows them to become accepted members of their kennel community. For dogs, just like people, one sideways glance, one twitch of the ear, or one slightly raised lip can say a thousand words.

Dogs understand things.

Dogs understand other dogs better than people understand dogs.

Dogs understand people better than people understand people.

The reason? Maybe it's because people talk so much that they don't have time to listen.

Dogs can't talk so they listen a lot.

That's why dogs understand things better than people.

—Don Beland
Veteran Musher/Philosopher

The body language of dominance is a raised tail, upright ears, and a little prancing.

Dominance

Sled dogs establish a hierarchy in the kennel that is essential to the harmony of the group. Every dog knows where he fits. This ladder of authority is reconfigured every time a new dog joins the group or a youngster comes of age.

Dominant dogs insist that people show them deference and respect. When they are challenged, they indicate their displeasure by a sudden cross look, by showing their teeth, or by growling. In this way they will announce their opinion of a situation long before engaging in a physical confrontation.

43

Nanook

"Nanook may have saved my life and the lives of two snowmobilers," Bob Klaesges asserts. The retired musher, former dog race promoter, and northern Minnesota resort owner was talking about the big, all-white Alaskan husky who was a great puller and one of his personal favorites.

When not racing, Bob hooks up small dog teams to pull him up the nearby Kawishiwi River to fish for walleye and northern pike, which is what he was doing with his lead dog Nanook one fateful day. "While I was fishing, the weather changed and a blizzard blew in, blotting out the world. Total whiteout. I had no idea where the trail was, but I did know that there were some dangerous spots near the rapids and down by the dam where the river wasn't frozen. And I knew it might not be a good idea to stay out all night if the temperature went down. With no other choice, I packed up my fishing tackle, climbed on the runners, and just said to my lead dog: 'Take me home, Nanook,' and we started out into the blinding snow storm. A short way down river we came upon two snowmobilers who were parked on the ice. Their trail had also drifted over, and they didn't know where they were. On top of that, it was now growing dark."

Klaesges explained to them that he was relying on Nanook to find the way out and that if they wanted to be alive in the morning they had better follow. The snowmobilers agreed. Bob took a flashlight out of his packsack, lashed it to shine backward from the sled, flipped the switch so the snowmobilers could follow the light, and yelled "Hike!" to Nanook. Unerringly, the dog followed trail through miles of darkness and swirling snow to the Klaesges' resort on Farm Lake where Shirley, Bob's wife, was worriedly waiting. In moments they were within the warm, lighted interior of the lodge, drinking hot coffee and laughing about their ordeal. Only Nanook knew how close they may have come to open water, and Nanook wasn't talking.

Authority vs. Position

Dominant dogs don't always make good lead dogs. Some of the best lead dogs are submissive in the pack, but they are extremely intelligent and can withstand the pressure of being chased by the whole team.

A dog's mouth is an important communication tool. They often show submission by licking or nuzzling another dog's chin. They'll do the same with people, too!

A **submissive** dog shows his lower status in a variety of ways. A dog who hangs his head, lowers his tail slightly, puts his ears back, or rolls over is demonstrating either fear or a fervent wish to have other dogs and you approve of him. Such dogs, who always aim to please, make great friends if they are encouraged by a little regular reassurance.

Droopy tails and ears can also mean that the dog is ill.

47

Teamwork with Teamwords

Somewhere in the ancient lore of dog sledding, perhaps embedded in errant press reports of the Alaskan gold rush days, an image appears of a fur-clad driver cracking a whip over his dogs and shouting: "Mush!" It didn't happen.

The part about the driver dressed in furs is largely correct. Some drivers used to crack a whip at times. And drivers are called "mushers," but they will all deny ever yelling "Mush!" To get the team underway, the driver pulls up the snow hook, throws it on the sled, grips the driving bow firmly, and yells "**Hike!**" or maybe "OK," "Go," or "Yeah." But never "Mush!" And that's if they have to yell anything at all and the dogs are not already barreling down the trail at full speed upon the release of the snow hook.

Once underway, the only real control the driver has over the team is by voice signals. That's why clear communication and a keen affinity between the lead dog and the musher is so crucial.

At 20 miles per hour the team may be called upon to choose the left or right fork in the trail, turn down a side road, or simply veer over to make room for a passing team. "**Gee**" (pronounced like the letter in the alphabet) signals the lead dog to go right, and "**Haw**" signals the lead dog to go left. If the driver wants the team to continue straight past an intersection, "**On by**" is the command most often used. The same words should move a team past another on the trail without incident.

Teams will slow down in response to "**Easy!**" In order to bring the team to a halt, the call is "**Whoa!**" accompanied by a hard lean on the foot brake. Once the team is stopped, the snow hook or brush hook is jammed into the hard pack or snagged onto a sturdy sapling or bush to hold the team while the driver untangles lines or perhaps even swings the team around to face in a different direction.

Mushers occasionally use an assortment of other words, mostly unprintable, when the team does something crazy like going after a squirrel that crosses the path or veering off course to challenge a moose.

Most of the time, however, these six basic commands are all that is needed.

TEAM WORDS

Hike—Let's go!

Gee—Turn right

Haw—Turn left

Easy—Slow down

On by—Pass another team

Whoa—Stop!

Howling

Dogs howl for many reasons—to express exuberance or hunger, to warn of an intruder, or just for the fun of it. Many kennels start and end each day with a spontaneous group howl. Perhaps this is just a way for them to mark time. Mushers can distinguish between dogs' voices, even in large kennels, and can often interpret the reason for the howl by the tone and cadence of the song. For dogs, however, howling is as contagious as yawning. Sometimes they seem to howl for no reason other than to celebrate the pure joy of making noise!

When Nellie Didn't Want to Run...

Sports fans sometimes get irritated by athletes who act like prima donnas, who throw tantrums, snarl at the crowd, or act like spoiled brats. In most of these instances, it is possible to trace the problem to an official's call, an undetected foul, a conflict with a coach or manager, a contract dispute, an insult shouted from the stands, or some other incident that set the athlete off.

Although the sled dog is also an athlete, it is often very difficult to determine what makes a dog throw a tantrum, since the dog cannot easily verbally communicate his displeasure to the musher.

Here's an example.

The legendary Dr. Roland Lombard, a skilled dog sledding veterinarian, first established his credentials in 1930 as a high school senior in New Hampshire. He won the Laconia World Championship with two Siberian huskies, a half-cocker, half-collie lead dog named Bucky, plus several canines of undetermined ancestry. Lombard nosed out some of the best mushers in North America to win $1,400—money that he put toward his veterinarian studies. Doc went on to win the Fairbanks North American race six times and the Anchorage Fur Rendezvous race seven times, but he was also remembered for his troubles in the 1973 All American race held in Minnesota.

He had purchased a famous lead dog, Nellie, from Alaskan musher George Attla. The dog had won dozens of major races and had been written up in Reader's Digest magazine. At the 1973 race, the timer was giving the final countdown: "Ten...nine...eight..." as Doc Lombard's team stood in the starting chute straining to go.

The announcer had just given a colorful account of Nellie's accomplishments from her first racing days with Attla to her present fame as Lombard's leader. Hundreds of race fans crowding around the starting area craned their necks for a better look. Doc Lombard, dressed in his fur-collared parka, tensed on the runners of his sled, ready to rip.

"Seven...six...five...four...three...two...one...GO!"

At that point, Nellie lay down on the snow.

Momentarily stunned, Lombard recovered and shouted, but Nellie had decided it was not time to run. She lay with her muzzle on her paws, stretched out on the hard packed surface, and calmly eyed the crowd, which was now convulsed in laughter.

Lombard slammed in his snow hook and ran to the head of his team, pulled Nellie to her feet, shouted a terse word of encouragement, ran back to the sled, and yelled: "Hike!"

Nellie sat down.

The clock was running. Valuable seconds were ticking off. By now, race fans were flopping all over the snow in mirth, slapping their legs, wiping away tears. Lombard dashed back to the head of his team, pulled Nellie to her feet, yelled some words that were drowned out by the laughter, sprinted back to his sled, and yelled: "Hike!"

This time, Nellie shot down the chute, and the team tore out of sight in a cloud of flying snow crystals. Doc lost that race by a mere one second.

What possessed Nellie to lie down in the chute? No one will ever know for sure, but some veteran mushers said it might have been the hubbub around the starting area, the huge crowd pressing in to see the famous dog and driver. Maybe with all the noise Nellie simply did not hear the "Go!" signal. Or maybe Nellie, like some great human athletes, just stubbornly wanted a few moments of attention.

Whatever the reason, this unpredictable behavior is now a piece of sled dog history.

Photographic Memory

Sue Hendrickson Schurke owns and operates Wintergreen Designs, a company specializing in anoraks and other winter apparel. She spent her first winter in northern Minnesota working for Arctic adventurer Will Steger. It was while working for Will that she met her husband Paul. At that time Paul and Will were mushing guides, taking groups on sled dog camping trips into the Boundary Waters.

"Once we took a dog team to Basswood Lake, down through Crooked Lake to Lac La Croix, and returned home through Hustler, Oyster, and Beartrap Creek. When we hit Crooked Lake, we found a place to camp in the shelter of a spruce swamp, out of the wind and with plenty of firewood.

"Our lead dog, Midas, was a hard worker but had a mind of his own. Three years later we were guiding some students from St. Thomas College on the same route— only this time we hit Crooked Lake late in the day in a roaring storm.

Fine snow was gusting in a howling wind, blotting out our vision. We were struggling along in deep drifts of snow, barely moving, exhausted, cold, and hungry. We couldn't recognize any landmarks along the shore but knew we had to make camp somewhere and soon. But where?

"Suddenly Midas stopped and refused to follow the trail. Instead, he led the dog team into a clump of trees, out of the wind, and sat down. This was quite unusual, but no amount of urging could get him moving. In resignation, Paul and I looked around in the blowing snow, and it dawned on us that Midas was sitting on the same spot, in the same spruce swamp, where we had camped three winters earlier. Somehow Midas had zeroed in on the site and stopped. Perhaps he remembered through some lingering scent. Over the years we have been astounded at what dogs remember. They have senses and powers of memory that are beyond human understanding."

Ten Dogs and a Raven

Don Beland, a veteran musher from northern Minnesota, has firsthand experience with the mystery of dogs.

"Anyone who has ever owned a dog—any kind of dog—knows there is some kind of communication between people and dogs. Dogs can sense what people are thinking, even what people are doing, without even seeing the people involved. If I am in the house cutting up meat to mix with their food, the dogs know it and start to bark. Without seeing me, they know when I am getting harnesses ready to go for a run and will be up and ready when I walk into the yard.

"Dogs not only have this sixth sense with people, but they communicate with other wildlife as well. Take the raven for instance. Ravens and wolves often work together as hunters. The raven is an important symbol to many northern Native Americans and is universally respected as a very wise and knowing bird. I imagine dogs also respect ravens.

"In a race I ran up at Tok, Alaska, one of the sharp turns in the course wasn't well marked. I was tearing down the trail and happened to be out in front so I didn't have another team to follow and couldn't see the turn. As I approached this spot, I noticed a raven in a tree by the side of the trail. Suddenly, it swooped ahead of the dogs and flew directly down the trail drawing the attention of my dogs. Then the raven banked its wings and made the sharp, unmarked turn on the trail. The dogs made the same turn. The raven flew on ahead and landed on a post near the finish. When we came in, the raven was perched on the post staring at us, nodding his head up and down like he expected us to come in exactly like we did.

"We won the race. You figure that one out."

Training

Easy!

The command that tells the team to slow down or ignore a distraction and keep on the trail

The bond between a sled dog and the musher begins when the dog is a puppy. Even untrained sled dog puppies naturally want to lean into the harness and pull. But it's important that each pup becomes accustomed to wearing a harness and responding to human commands, so that as the dog matures, it can channel that energy into pulling as part of a team.

It is said that a puppy will never forget what it learns during the first 17 weeks of life. The relationship between dog and musher is nurtured and strengthened over the years by extensive training, feeding, and living side-by-side. Regular training reinforces this connection as the team establishes its rhythm, gets physical exercise, and, most importantly, has fun together. Mushers contend that the strength of this bond inspires the best teams to persevere through grueling races and adverse conditions.

Early Training

Training can begin when the dogs are still pups by getting them used to going for short walks while wearing a harness. Children can help teach the dogs key skills, like pulling and following each other, that are essential to productive teamwork later in life.

It is nearly impossible to teach a sled dog to heel—it's just not in its nature.

Non-Winter Activities

If sled dogs exercise strenuously in the summer, they are at risk of overheating because of their dense coats of fur. The serious training, therefore, begins in the fall when temperatures cool down, but well before the snow flies. When there is no snow, the team is often hitched to a 4-wheeler, which it pulls down a gravel roadway. It's a strange sight to see, but it affords the team excellent pre-season practice.

Sled dogs are naturally-born pullers. It's in their genes. As dogs mature, this instinct is honed by a wide variety of pulling exercises.

First Run

Once accustomed to the harness, adolescent dogs between six and nine months of age are formally introduced to their teammates and taken on their first trial run. Over time, the young sled dogs are moved into the position on the team that suits them best. On this first excursion, their enthusiasm is usually quite high because they're finally a part of the group.

Harnessing

After a dog is harnessed, he will often rear up on his hind legs in excitement and "hop" to the sled. This use of two legs rather than four makes it easier for the handler to manage the dog. Like taking a car out of four-wheel drive, it reduces the superior strength and balance that a dog enjoys with all four paws on the ground. Many a handler has been toppled and dragged through the snow when he could not control the dog's enthusiasm!

Harnessing and hooking up a large team must be done quickly. Otherwise, chaos results as the excited dogs jump around and get tangled. Usually the lead dogs are connected first and told to "stay tight." Their ability to stand in one place and keep the gang line taut while the other dogs are hitched up helps the musher get the rest of the team ready.

Hitching up the Team

All dogs are harnessed to a single **gang line**, made of polypropylene rope or a cable. The gang line runs the length of the whole team, extending from the back of the lead dog's harness to the sled itself. The rest of the dogs run alongside the gang line and are doubly connected to it with a **neck line** that is attached to their collars and a **tug line** that runs from the back of their harnesses.

Gang lines, when taut, are designed to provide the proper distance between dogs. Attaching the dogs in front and back also makes it difficult for them to turn around and argue or mate with their neighbors. Because of the high adrenaline charge the dogs experience during running, fights have been known to erupt—even between teams of dogs that have known each other for years. If a dog stumbles, or the team collides with another team, a thrashing, snarling tangle can occur in a split second. Veteran mushers know how to jump into the middle of a tangle, heave dogs to the right and left, roll them over, and shove them out of the way to straighten out the lines and get the team going again.

Harnesses are made of reinforced webbing. Available in many sizes, they are designed to hug the body so that no chafing occurs during running. They should fit snugly and comfortably so that most of the "pulled" weight is borne by the dog's sturdy shoulder and chest area.

Team Positions

Sled dogs are strategically positioned just like members of a football team, each playing a crucial role.

Lead dogs are easy to identify because they're out front. Teams have either one or two dogs in lead at any given time, sometimes rotating dogs into and out of this position over the course of long races. The lead dogs set the running pace, respond to directional commands, and generally act as the musher's "right arm." Running in lead requires the most emotional stamina of all positions. Lead dogs must be willing to be "chased" by teammates—an intimidating task for some! Not surprisingly, some dogs simply refuse the honor of leading by putting their tails between their legs and not moving.

Two **point dogs** follow directly behind the lead dogs. Sometimes mushers put apprentice or substitute lead dogs in the point position to help them gain lead experience. Point dogs also respond to voice commands, sometimes correcting an error made by a lead dog who isn't listening.

The pair of dogs directly in front of the sled are called **wheel dogs** because of their proximity to the "vehicle." They are usually chosen for their brute strength and stamina and are the kennel's best athletes. Dogs in this position should also have quick reflexes because they are most affected by erratic sled movements. Commonly, two young males are placed in this position. Too young and immature to lead, they are safely placed in the wheel position where they can't really do any harm.

The dogs located in the middle of the lineup, making the bulk of the team, are called **swing dogs** or **team dogs**. Teams of five dogs have no swing dogs, whereas teams of seven have two swing dogs. Teams of nine have four swing dogs, and so on.

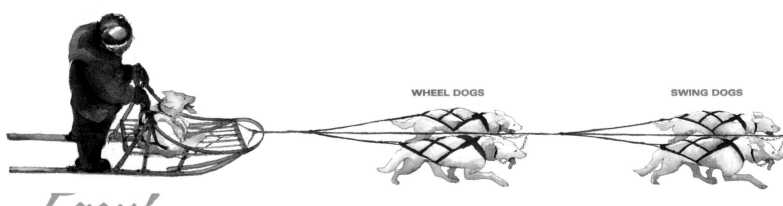

WHEEL DOGS   SWING DOGS

Lead Dogs

Lead dogs are picked through a process of trial and error. Mushers look for a dog with rare leadership qualities—stamina, obedience, and intelligence. Most lead dogs are born, not made.

A good runner is tenacious, enthusiastic, and cooperative. Some mushers say that many of the best sled dogs are female.

SWING DOG

POINT DOGS

LEAD DOGS

GANG LINE

TUGLINE

Getting Along

The surest way to minimize tension and posturing between running mates is to pair a male with a female who is not in heat. Since many mushers breed their dogs, they don't spay or neuter many in the kennel. Staying alert to which dogs are in heat is an essential skill that becomes second nature when planning the lineup of a team.

After they are harnessed together, the paired dogs are given a short chance to chat and nuzzle. This gentle introduction helps make sure that the two dogs will run well together without distracting growls and nips.

Spitz

Spitz was a seventy-pound, five-year-old husky when Harry and Mary Lambirth acquired him from veteran musher Gary Paulsen. Harry and Mary, famed canoe guides and angling experts, paddle and portage the Boundary Waters canoe country along the Minnesota-Ontario border during the summer. In winter they snug down in their woodland cabin near Blackduck, Minnesota, where they prepare their dog teams for mid-distance races.

"Spitz was a real piece of work," Harry noted. "Somewhere in his early life he must have had a bad experience with a man, somebody who beat him or mistreated him. He didn't like men. He got along fine with women, and when Mary harnessed him she had no problems. But when I drove him, there was usually a confrontation and the dog and I had to reach an understanding of who was in charge."

"Spitz would work with men if he had to," Mary added, "but he loved women. He was a special dog in that he had neither the ability nor the build to be a great lead dog, but what he lacked in strength, he made up for with heart and desire."

"Years ago we were in a race that followed Alaska's Yanert River," Harry recalled with a smile. "It's a glacial river near Denali National Park, a river with a strong current, with overflow and sometimes shifting ice. It was spring, and the river was opening up. Luckily, my team was one of the last to get underway, so other teams were ahead of me to test the ice.

"One thing about veteran lead dogs, they know instinctively if the musher is experienced or a beginner, and Spitz knew I was the latter. He also understood that we had to cross to the other side of the river at some point and that I would have no idea which ice was safe."

Unknown to Harry, one musher and his team had already fallen through the ice downriver. Luckily, Harry had enough knowledge of dogs in general, and Spitz in particular, to allow the dog to make the decisions. Whenever Harry saw what looked like solid ice and shouted a command to cut across, Spitz would instead continue straight downriver. Suddenly, Spitz made his decision, aimed for a narrow ice bridge and took Harry, the team, and the sled across the current without incident.

Mary smiled. "Your first lead dog is always a special dog," she noted. "The first thing you learn to accept is that they know a lot more than you do. And they know that you are inexperienced, but they will still do everything they can to help you."

Like many mushers, Harry and Mary have limited resources but unlimited determination. They are slowly building up their team as they hone their skills. They now compete in three or four major races every year.

Harry and Mary have developed close ties with their dogs, an esprit de corps, and a comradeship which is evident when they race. Most importantly, they've learned when to trust their dogs' intuition—even when it contradicts their own.

Raw Power

A team of sled dogs can pull a six thousand-pound truck out of a ditch. The power of the team is barely contained by a mere snow hook or foot brake. Instead, the collective energy is held in check or unleashed by a relationship of mutual respect between the musher and the team. When a musher loses a team, it's usually because the musher let go or fell off, not because the team deliberately disobeyed.

The Sled

Today most racing sleds weigh less than forty pounds and are about eight feet long, while freight sleds are longer, heavier, and a great deal more sturdy. Both types are the result of a long evolution of form and function. The Cree Indians of the north perfected the toboggan sled design with an uplifted snout, useful for a rocky and forested terrain. Natives of Alaska were the first to use a freight sled with runners. Their dog teams ran long distances over relatively flat ice and gained efficiency by minimizing the sled's gliding surface. Inuit people ingeniously fashioned sleds out of frozen bundles of sealskin wrapped around fish and had the dogs pull the bundles home! The modern day racing sled, which is still being improved each year, has this rich history to thank for its efficient design.

Racing sleds are handcrafted of white ash, hickory, or birch strips in designs perfected by centuries of use and, regardless of subtle style differences, share some common characteristics. The typical sled is lightweight, flexible, and surprisingly strong, but it possesses all the grace and fine craftsmanship of a work of art.

They are also fairly fragile. When the snow hook doesn't hold and the team takes off on their own and crashes, the sled usually ends up broken and splintered.

Nomenclature of a Sled

Brush Bow—The curved, oval-shaped section that acts like a bumper when going through weeds or brush. Made of durable plastic or steamed and bent wood, usually wrapped with rawhide, it is an integral part of the sled, containing anchor points for connecting the gang line.

Basket—The framed-in space behind the brush bow and between the runners where freight, passengers, and injured or sick dogs are carried. Often this area is enclosed with canvas or nylon to create a large, windproof bag.

Snow Hook (also called the **Brush Hook**)—The large steel hook that is connected to the sled with a section of rope and acts like an anchor. The hook is sharply pointed and can be driven into the snow to lock the sled and team in place while the musher straightens out lines or makes repairs. The hook can also be snagged onto a sapling or a clump of brush, hence its name.

Driving Bow (also called the **Handle Bar**)— The erect, curved strip of rawhide-covered wood that the musher grips in order to stay on the sled while driving the team.

Foot Brake—The hinged, flat section of toothed metal that can be pressed down with one foot to dig into the snow. It helps the team stop and also slows the sled on downhills to prevent it from running over the dogs.

Foot Boards—The plastic or rubber-covered slabs of wood fastened to the back of runners on which the musher stands.

Runners—The longitudinal strips on each side of the sled, usually shod with teflon or aluminum to prevent wear and maximize speed.

Stanchions—The vertical bars of wood that connect the handle bar with the runners and form the frame for the back of the basket.

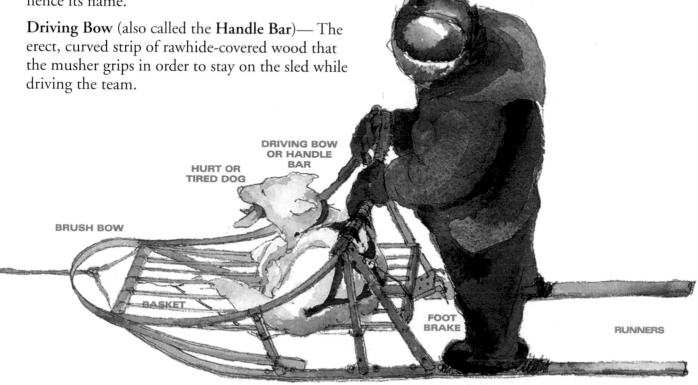

DRIVING BOW OR HANDLE BAR

HURT OR TIRED DOG

BRUSH BOW

BASKET

FOOT BRAKE

RUNNERS

STANCHION   FOOT BOARDS

Don't Let Go!

"The first time I saw the Boundary Waters I was a youngster on a church group canoe trip," Paul Schurke recalled as we sat in a small restaurant in Ely, Minnesota. Outside, snow swirled down the street. "We camped on Basswood Lake, and I just couldn't get enough of all that beautiful country. I was hooked."

Paul returned to the Boundary Waters a number of times, often as a leader for canoe trips sponsored by St. John's College. "One of the first Ely people I got to know was a crusty old character named Checker Hillman. I told Checker that I had seen the Boundary Waters in the summer but that I wanted to spend some time out there in the winter. Checker directed me to Pickett's Lake where he said a guy named Will Steger was training sled dogs."

After that first meeting, Paul went to work for Will, learning the skills required to run and care for sled dogs. "From the beginning, Will had a saying he tried to impress on my mind. It was that no matter what, a musher never lets go of his sled. I never really understood what this was all about until one overcast winter day he sent me up an old logging railroad grade to give the dogs a workout and bring back a sled load of firewood for the stove. Late in the afternoon I stopped to stack some wood in the sled but I didn't tie up the team. Suddenly the dogs took off and I followed in a dead run, yelling at them to stop.

"Of course, the dogs didn't stop. Instead they sprinted up the trail, around a bend in the dense forest, and vanished in the direction of Basswood Lake. Eventually, I stumbled onto the shore, and stared at the dog tracks that disappeared into the snow aiming toward Canada.

"It was starting to get dark, and I was terrified that I had lost Will's team. I peered out into the gloom, wondering how I could return and face Will without the dogs." Paul paused, remembering his feelings of panic.

"The dog track led past a truck parked near the edge of the bay, and as I came out on the ice I spied a tiny speck in the distance. I thought it might be just a big rock. But there seemed to be more to it, some small movement. So I started in that direction, hoping it could be the sled and perhaps some of the dogs. As I got closer I made out the sled and the whole team sitting in a circle on the ice. In the middle of the circle was an elderly ice fisherman hunched over a hole. The dogs were staring intently at this old man and did not move as I approached, stepped on the sled, and grabbed the handles. At this point, the old-timer glared at me and snarled: 'Who is going to pay for all my fish that your dogs ate?'

"Apparently the runaway team had smelled the fish lying on the ice, zeroed in on the fisherman, and proceeded to gulp down his entire catch. Then they sat down to wait for him to catch some more. He was afraid of the dogs and didn't know what to do. So he just sat there."

Paul was overjoyed to find his team intact, and once he had the dogs clearly under control,

Easy! **TRAINING**

he apologized profusely for the missing fish. "That old guy never cracked a smile," Paul said. "I pointed out that I couldn't replace the fish but since it was growing dark, the least I could do was give him a ride back to his truck. He still looked mad, but he rolled up his tackle, climbed onto the sled, and rode back to the truck. I was so happy to get the dog team back, I never did find out the fisherman's name, but his fish certainly saved me a lot of embarrassment.

"Eventually, the dogs took me back down the railroad line and into Will Steger's camp. I never again lost control of a dog team."

On by!

Racing

The command that tells the team to pass another team or obstacle

Mushing can be purely recreational or very competitive. Over one hundred races of all lengths and types are organized each year in the United States and Canada alone. Naturally, most of them are scattered across the northern regions. International dog sled associations also have a strong presence and sponsor races in the Baltic nations, Western Europe, New Zealand, Australia, and South America.

Unlike many other sports, in mushing men and women compete on equal footing. For example, Minnesotan Jamie Nelson is a champion in this sport, which was once thought to be the province of only the most rugged northwoods men. She stands tall with other champion mushers such as Dee Dee Jonrowe, Susan Butcher, Martin Buser, Doug Swingley, Tim White, and Libby Riddles.

Types of Races

The well-known 1,100-mile Iditarod race across Alaska is considered to be the "SuperBowl" of long-distance dog racing. The 500-mile John Beargrease across northeastern Minnesota is one of the premiere races in the lower forty-eight states, but more than ten races of similar length are held each winter. Mid-distance races, of 150 miles or less, occur almost every weekend throughout the winter, and several hundred sprint races of 10 to 20 miles offer almost endless options for race watching. Stage races of 5 to 40 miles long are held over a number of days, usually over the same course each day, with teams winning prizes for the best combined time.

In addition, close to one hundred organizations and businesses across the country offer weekend and extended wilderness dog sled expeditions for the general public.

RACES

Long distance/marathon—
150 + miles, usually overnight

Mid-distance—20 to 150 miles, usually completed in one day

Sprint—10 to 20 miles

Stage—5 to 40 miles, run each day for several days

Traveling to Races

In some cases, when traveling long distances to a race, sled dogs are flown in individual dog boxes. More frequently, however, they ride in specially-made, condominium-style boxes fitted to the backs of pickup trucks. The designs of these boxes become trademarks of kennels and are readily identified on the road. Once the team arrives at its destination, or if the group stops for a rest, dogs are unloaded individually and hitched up to very short tethers staked out around the truck. The dogs can then stretch their muscles, greet their neighbors, and perhaps get booties put on before the harnessing begins.

How Many Dogs Do You Need?

Sprint racing teams consist of up to twenty-eight dogs but travel only a few miles. Teams involved in marathon races, either mid- or long-distance, are usually limited to sixteen to eighteen dogs. Smaller teams of three or four dogs are often used for recreational trips. Weight-pulling contests can feature a single dog or a small team.

On snow, one dog can pull up to one thousand pounds for a short distance, and a freight dog team can pull several thousand pounds. Since they must run quickly over great distances, racing teams are most effective when pulling loads of five hundred pounds or less.

A team's performance also depends on trail conditions. Naturally, it is easier to pull any load over a hard-packed trail than one covered with freshly-fallen snow. Volunteer snowmobilers often pack trails the day before a race to improve conditions.

FEED SUPPLIED

73

Funny Liked to Barrel Home

Until 1986, Myron Angstman had never won a race, although he had tried the Iditarod once and the Kuskowin 300 three times. An attorney in Bethel, Alaska, Myron had migrated from Minnesota, established his law office, and set about assembling a dog team at his Old Friendly Dog Farm. His lead dog was an aging ten-year-old veteran named Funny, a throwback to the village dogs of the '50s and '60s with barely enough speed to keep up with most of the teams in the '80s. However, Funny did know how to pour on the steam when it was necessary.

About six weeks before the Kuskowin, Myron took the team on an extended training run, staying overnight at a distant village. On the way back, Funny came up lame and had to be carried home on the sled.

"At his age—ten—I assumed he was done for the season and probably for his career," the musher explained. At home, Myron tied the dog out and just about forgot about him for a couple of weeks.

"After three weeks I noticed that he was looking somewhat better, although still limping," Myron continued. "I decided that since he was an old leader, probably ready for retirement, I should turn him loose and allow him the run of the yard. I often do this because older dogs tend to stay close to home, and they deserve their freedom.

"My office is located right at home so I could keep an eye on Funny. As race day approached, it appeared that his gait was better and he limped only slightly as he walked around the yard. From experience, I knew that some dogs were able to run in a team even if they started out limping. After a few miles the limp would disappear as the muscles warmed up.

"On Saturday before the race, I was making my final preparations. I sorely missed Funny, and because he looked almost ready, I hooked him up for a training run. We went about fifteen miles, and, true to form, he started out slowly but came home strong.

"I harnessed him up again on Monday for a ten-mile run and pronounced him ready to race. Old timers told me that old dogs don't need much training, and even though Funny had only completed two runs in about six weeks, I decided to take him to the Kuskowin 300. To give Funny a little extra rest, I let him sleep in the house.

"On the night before the race, I snapped awake at three in the morning to find that Funny had jumped into bed with my wife and me. He was sitting on his haunches at my feet, staring at me. To this day he is the only sled dog who's ever been in my bed, and I have often wondered what he was trying to tell me."

Because of Funny's injuries, Myron decided to carry him in the sled for the first part of the race, saving his strength for the last part. During the first fifty miles, the trail followed the icy winter truck road parallel to the Kuskowin River. Funny sat up in the sled with only his neck showing above the sled bag, casually watching. The dog team seemed to be doing well, and things looked promising. When they stopped for a rest, Myron opened the bag. Funny hopped out of the sled, barking to go, as he was harnessed up with the team.

"With Funny now in the lead," Myron recalled, "things began to happen. True to form, he started each run out slow, but would increase his speed, coming into the next checkpoint moving strong. Breaks were only twenty-five to thirty minutes at each checkpoint, but even so his shoulder would stiffen and he would be limping as we started out.

At Kalsag we were running about eighth, still one hundred miles from Bethel. We were fourth as we came into Tulusak, fifty miles from the finish line. By now, Funny was clearly aware that home was not far away. He limped out of Tulusak but within a mile was going strong. We caught the third place team handled by famous Eskimo musher Herbie Nuyukpuk from Shishmaref. Grimly intent on the trail ahead, Funny hardly glanced at the other team as we went past."

Myron never did see the second place team, which had somehow gotten lost after coming out of Aniak. Twenty miles from the finish, the first place team driven by the legendary George Attla came into view. From that point on, the lead changed ten times as they approached Bethel almost neck and neck.

"Old Funny was running strong as we headed onto the wide river for the last three miles to town, but he was tucked in behind Attla's sled and didn't seem to want to pass. Now the town was well in sight. Six hundred yards from the finish line, Funny realized exactly how close he was to the end and began lunging to get there."

Race movies show old Funny limping badly as he gamely crossed the finish line in first place in what was one of the closest and most gutsy performances ever for a ten-year-old lead dog.

"It was a fitting end to Funny's racing career. He never completed another race. We turned him loose to run the yard, and he lived on another five winters. In his last years, he developed a fondness for sleeping in the house at the Old Friendly Dog Farm, a reward he justly deserved."

Feisty

Myron Angstman was more than a little miffed. He had been leading the last leg of the 1986 Beargrease 500 all the way to the final checkpoint at Beaver Bay and had pulled up for a short rest when the second-place sled whipped past him. By the time Myron got his team on the trail again he couldn't quite catch up. He had to settle for second place. And second is not good enough for the Alaskan musher. He returned in 1987, seeking to avenge his previous loss.

"I had a big problem, however," Myron pointed out. "My lead dog, Feisty, was difficult to handle. On the trail, she had a mind of her own. What's more, whenever she got loose, she was virtually impossible to catch. The only one who could corner her was my daughter."

Myron flew his team into Duluth, Minnesota, for the 1987 race and stayed with a friend.

"Two days before the race, we were on our last training run using the Beargrease Trail itself, north of Duluth. We hitched up in an area where a lot of mushers run, and because I had one of the few Alaskan teams, several local mushers came over to size up my operation.

"Most of them knew I had set a new record in winning the 1986 Kuskowin 300 so they naturally expected I had a hot shot team. On the other hand, my dogs were widely known for their slow start, and this practice run was no exception. In addition, during the first few miles, Feisty occasionally tried to bolt off the trail. With several spectators watching, I was hoping she would outdo herself and run steadily, but Feisty had other ideas. Three hundred yards away from the dog truck, she made an abrupt left turn downhill and into a ditch by the highway. It took me twenty minutes to get the team untangled and once more underway. I am sure the mushers watching would have taken bets that I was going to finish far back in the pack during the race."

He continued on with the training run, but instead of improving, things got worse. When Myron got his team back to their lodging, Feisty got loose in the fenced-in yard as she was being unloaded from the truck. Myron and his friend spent the rest of the afternoon trying to catch the dog but without any luck. If they couldn't catch the dog, Myron knew he would have no leader and no team in the race. In desperation, he phoned his daughter who happened to be visiting grandparents in Princeton, Minnesota, before coming up to watch the race. Myron begged his daughter to cut her visit short and help round up Feisty.

In the meantime, he watched Feisty carefully as they chased her around the yard. They noticed that she occasionally dashed through a gap between two garages. Since the gap was only about three feet wide, they set up a plan so that when she ran into the corridor again, they blocked off both ends and cornered her. It took over an hour to get her to go between the two garages again, but when she did, they managed to get the barricades in place. As soon as Feisty saw that she was cornered, she rolled over on her back, feet up, in the classic submissive pose.

Myron's daughter arrived after Feisty had been captured, but he felt better just having her around. The next morning, she helped her dad hook up his team as the race got underway.

Once again Feisty was slow starting out, and most of the other teams were well ahead of Myron as they came into the halfway point at Grand Portage. But on the return run to Duluth, Feisty kicked into gear and began passing one team after another. In the end, they overtook and edged out all other teams by fifteen minutes to win the race.

Myron laughs as he remembers the circumstances leading up to that event. "I doubt if anyone else ever won the Beargrease 500 with a lead dog that ran away and had to be trapped the day before the race."

Behind the Scenes

Handlers and volunteers provide indispensable support to all mushing events. At the starting lineup of a race, the dogs' level of excitement and tension reaches chaotic proportions. Mushers assign at least one person to hold the gangline between every pair of dogs, and even with this many assistants, keeping the team in one place is difficult. Dogs bark and howl exuberantly and lunge against their harnesses with mounting frenzy. However, when the start signal is given and the volunteers step away, a sudden magical hush falls upon the team as they rocket forward and begin the race.

On by! RACING

Racing Safety and Regulations

Today's race organizers place the highest priority on the safety and care of the dogs. A team of veterinarians oversees the events and conducts both pre-race examinations and spot checkups throughout the race. Random blood and urine samples are also collected before and after racing to make sure no dog shows traces of performance-inducing or illness-suppressing drugs.

In long-distance races, each team starts the marathon with a minimum of seven and a maximum of eighteen dogs. Each musher's gear is checked to ensure he has the proper equipment along. This gear typically includes:

- two headlamps

- an emergency gangline cutter

- a knife

- fire starters and cooking equipment

- a sleeping bag

- one or two sets of booties for each dog (that's 128 booties for a sixteen-dog team!)

- snowshoes

- a first aid kit

- an axe

- a sled dog bag to hold an injured dog

- emergency flares

- dog food

Collision in the Sub-Zero

International Falls, Minnesota, likes to bill itself as "The Icebox of the Nation," and it often lives up to its reputation.

For instance, thermometers read 41° below zero at the start of the 1996 Esslinger Dog Sled Race. As an added complication, the race had what is known as a "Klondike Start." In a Klondike Start, the dog teams are tied to the musher's truck bumpers and the mushers are in sleeping bags with their boots off. At the start signal, mushers climb out of their bags, lace on their boots, pack their sleeping bags onto the sled basket, and untie the dogs before getting underway.

Minnesota drivers Steve Crittendon and Harry Lambirth were tied up almost side-by-side, both going out at the same time. This was Steve's first experience with the Klondike start, and he had trouble getting his boots on. When Harry's team took off, it ran right into Steve's, creating a massive tangle of snarling, biting dogs, twisted lines, and swearing mushers. Harry and Steve had anchored their sleds and were sorting out the mess when a third team came up behind both teams, running over and cutting Steve's anchor line. Sensing their sled was free

On by! RACING

at last, Steve's dogs lurched forward, further aggravating the tangle.

In the midst of this barking melee, a race official ran over to help and somehow managed to unhook one of Steve's dogs, which promptly began to circle on a dead run, barking at the pileup. Realizing he had to catch the dog and get it back in the harness or he would be disqualified, Steve sprinted and collared it. Meanwhile, Harry got his team untangled and took off. Steve, too, eventually straightened out his lines and got underway.

"The race course ran through town so that people could watch," Steve recalled. "Streets were barricaded to mark the route, but my team got confused with the noise and the crowd. I yelled 'gee!' and the dogs went 'haw!' smashing through a police barricade."

After a few detours, Steve got his team back on course and out of the city limits. "It was 41° below zero in town," he noted. "But the trail went downhill into a swamp which was at least ten degrees colder. It was like going from an icebox into a deep freezer. I held onto the sled, squatting behind the bag to keep out of the wind as much as possible. I could feel my fingers and my face starting to freeze.

"It was the longest, meanest seventy-five miles I ever rode on a dog sled. But even with all the trouble, our dogs did a heck of a job. Harry's team came in third, and mine finished fourth."

"It all depends on the dogs," Steve points out. "They are like top-notch athletes, but they can be temperamental. Sometimes your lead dogs will go 'haw!' when you yell 'gee!' just to try you out."

No Walk in the Park

Rarely does a musher have the luxury of simply standing on the runners and enjoying an effortless ride. While on the move, there is quite a lot a musher can do to assist the team and influence the sled's direction. On curves in the trail, the driver may shift her weight to the inside runner and lean inward to avoid tipping over. To make a sharp corner or avoid a tree, the musher may jump off the sled altogether and muscle it to the side while running behind.

A musher can help the team maintain speed by **pedaling**—using one foot to propel the sled along like a child pushing a scooter. This move is often used on a long flat area or while going uphill, where the extra effort takes weight off the sled and helps the dogs maintain their running speed. At the same time, the musher often shouts encouragement to the dogs, calling out their names and praising them.

Whips

Some early tales of dog sledding portray the driver controlling a team not only by voice commands, but also by the use of a long whip. This practice was more common a hundred years ago. In today's races, however, it is forbidden. A **signal whip,** only one meter long, may be allowed in some races. This whip makes a loud pop but does not actually touch any dog on the team. Whipping is not only abhorred by the public, it is equally despised by most mushers. Many consider the use of a whip to be a tacit admission that the driver has failed to build respect with the team and cannot motivate them without punishment.

When one team gains on another, the back driver calls "Trail." The lead team is required to pull over and help the other team to pass without tangling.

Moose Alert

Moose can present a formidable hazard on the trail, particularly in northern Minnesota, Canada, and Alaska. A face-off between a dog team and a moose is simply no contest. The moose always wins. In a contest between a musher and a moose, for that matter, the moose also wins unless the musher is packing a rifle. Moose often have short tempers, no fear of humans or dogs, and prefer to meet their enemies face-to-face. Unlike horses or mules, which kick with their back legs, moose kick with their front legs, producing a wallop like a lethal uppercut. A moose kick can cave in the whole rib cage of a dog or render its head into bloody pulp. Mushers are well aware of this and studiously avoid moose.

In races where moose are likely to be encountered, airplane spotters sometimes circle over the trails, and via radio, announce the location of any problem animals. Trail watchers can then notify passing mushers, and volunteers on snowmobiles may be dispatched to shag the moose away. "If we get a moose warning, we keep a sharp lookout ahead and to the side," one musher explained. "We try to slow the team, maintain control, and yell a lot. There is not much chance a moose will go out of its way to attack a team, but the moose can create a real problem if it comes out near the trail where the dogs can see it. Dogs tend to get very excited when they spot or smell a moose. It's in their genes, maybe in their wolf heritage, and unless the musher has tight control, the dogs may head right for the moose."

Dogs remember race trails from one year to the next. Some mushers purchase dogs for specific races and mix those who are familiar with a given trail with the rest of their team. In the dark, or in a blizzard, the dog's memory and perfect sense of direction can prevent the team from losing valuable time or, even worse, getting hopelessly lost.

Checkpoints

Layovers, or resting periods, of a specific time are required at prearranged checkpoints throughout a race.

Deciding how long to rest beyond the required minimum time becomes part of a musher's racing strategy. Each musher must carefully attend to the condition and fatigue level of the team before deciding to end a rest period and rejoin the race.

Checkpoints are also key opportunities for the musher to examine the team. He can leave, or "drop," tired or injured dogs at the checkpoints and go on with the race. Most distance races, however, require teams to finish with at least six of the original starting dogs.

Mushers can make arrangements to have food and assistance waiting at checkpoints. True to tradition, however, most races require that the mushers feed and care for their own teams personally, without the help of handlers or volunteers.

On by!

Prizes

Large headline races offer prize money of up to $400,000. Smaller races award less, and many simply offer a trophy and congratulations to both musher and dogs for a job well done. Rarely, however, do winnings compensate mushers for their expenses, unless they regularly place in the top three finishers. As a rule of thumb, most racers estimate the cost per year just for feeding each dog to be about $500 (that's $25,000 annually for a fifty-dog kennel). This, of course, does not include veterinary expenses or the cost of traveling to races in other states or countries.

Clothing

During a race, mushers have traditionally worn fur parkas, heavy wool pants, mukluks, wool socks, and mittens. Some now opt for synthetic fabrics that are superior in heat retention and moisture evaporation. They dress to fit the conditions. Because frostbite first attacks extremities like noses, eartips, and lips, parka hoods are often trimmed in fur to minimize the amount of wind passing the face,

In Your Blood...

"You can't buy just one sled dog," Don and Val Beland point out. "After you get one sled dog and harness it up, something happens. I don't know what it is, but then you have to get a couple more dogs. Pretty soon you have a team, and then you are into sled dogs. It gets into your blood and becomes your whole life." They should know.

Long time trapper, hunter, guide, and outfitter along the Ontario-Minnesota border, Don came to Minnesota in the 1950s from the Kankakee River country in Illinois, seeking some truly wild trapping country where he could move about with relative freedom. He settled in Ely, established a reputation as a woods-smart outdoorsman, and met his first sled dogs.

"A friend of mine had some big freight dogs," Don recalls. "I became fascinated with those dogs—with their strength, their loyalty, and the skill and teamwork required between the team and driver."

Don got a single dog from his friend and used it with a sled to haul supplies on his trapline. Five

RACING

decades later, he and his wife Val owned 175 sled dogs and created racing teams out of 100 to 125 of the best.

After years of competitive racing, both Don and Val have now retired from competition and are outfitting sled dog trips for people who wish to experience the exhilaration of a winter adventure in the crisp northern forest.

After almost fifty years it's still in their blood. And they claim there's no cure.

Sled Dog and Mushing Resources

International Sled Dog Racing Association
HC 86 Box 3380
Merrifield, MN 56465
phone 218-765-4297
http://uslink.net/~isdra

International Sled Dog Veterinary Medical Association
P.O. Box 543
Sylvania, OH 43615
phone 419-531-5589

Mush With Pride
P.O. Box 84915
Fairbanks, AK 99708

Mushing Magazine
P.O. Box 149
Ester, AK 99725-0149
phone 907-479-0454
fax 907-479-3137
http://www.mushing.com

Team and Trail
45 Sibley Road
Center Harbor, NH 03226-0128
phone 603-253-6265
fax 603-253-9513

Glossary

Alaskan husky—a mixed-breed husky, developed for endurance and racing performance

American Kennel Club (AKC)—a national organization that defines and maintains a registry of purebred dogs

Basket—the framed-in space on a racing sled where freight, passengers, or sick dogs are carried

Booties—paw coverings made of pile or felt, strapped on by Velcro, that protect a sled dog's feet

Brush bow—the curved, oval-shaped front section of a racing sled that acts like a bumper

Brush hook—the two-pronged sled anchor used to hold the team and sled in place, often dug into snow or snagged onto a sapling or bush

Driving bow—the erect, curved strip of rawhide-covered wood that the musher grips to stay on the sled

Easy!—the command that slows the pace of the team, or tells it to ignore a distraction and stay on the trail

Eskimo dog—burly, thick-furred sled dog of far arctic origin, often used on expeditions

Foot board—the slab of wood at the back of a sled, on which the musher stands

Foot brake—the toothed metal bar that slows the sled when pressed into the snow

Freight dog—sled dog used on expeditions and long adventure trips, known more for strength than speed

Gang line—the main artery of cable that attaches the dog team to the sled

Gee!—the command that tells the team to turn right

Handle bar—see Driving bow

Handler—a musher's assistant, responsible for the care and upkeep of the kennel

Harness—a system of reinforced webbing worn by a sled dog that distributes the pulled weight evenly across its shoulders and back

Haw!—the command that tells the team to turn left

Hike!—the command that tells the team, "Go!"

Iditarod—a 1,100-mile sled dog marathon race across Alaska, considered the "Super Bowl" of long-distance racing

John Beargrease Sled Dog Marathon—a dog sled race held annually in Northern Minnesota

Kennel—the group of dogs owned by a musher, also used to describe where the dogs live

Lead dog—the dog at the head of the team that sets the pace and guides the team along the trail

Malamute—a purebred dog with a strong physique, often used to pull freight

Marathon (long-distance) race—a sled dog race of over 150 miles, involving at least one overnight stay outdoors

Mid-distance race—a 20- to 150-mile race, usually completed in one day

Mukluks—soft boots made of hide or synthetic material, insulated with wool, originally worn by Eskimos

Musher—the driver of a dog sled

Neck line—the short line connecting a dog's collar to the gang line

On by!—the command that tells the team to go past another team or obstacle

Pedaling—a technique used by mushers to propel the sled along, much like a skateboard

Point dog—one of two dogs immediately behind the lead dog who also responds to directional commands

Racing dog—a sled dog specifically bred for speed

Runners—the long, ski-like strips, running the length of the sled, that allow it to glide over the snow

Signal whip—a small whip, about one meter in length, used to make a popping noise

Siberian husky—a medium-build, purebred dog with mask-like features and blue eyes, selectively bred for appearance and pulling ability

Snow hook—see Brush hook

Sprint race—a 10- to 20-mile, fast-paced race

Sprint racer—a sled dog capable of great speed, typically sleeker and smaller than a freight dog or a race dog

Stage race—a 5- to 40-mile race in which the same course is run over several days

Stanchions—the vertical bars of wood that connect the handle bar with the runners and form the back of the basket

Sweats—elastic, woven fabric wrapped around a dog's tendons to prevent post-race swelling

Swing dog—a sled dog located in the middle of the team lineup, usually making up the bulk of the team

Team dog—see Swing dog

Tug line—a short line connecting the back of a dog's harness to the gang line

Wheel dog—one of two dogs directly in front of the sled, often chosen for brute strength and stamina

Whoa!—the command that tells the team to stop